GRADE LEVEL: 2½ (MEDIUM EASY)

young symphonic band series

South Shore Soliloquy

By Robert Sheldon

This heartfelt elegy is dedicated to the life and memory of Dr. Gary Corcoran. His mentoring of so many music educators and students fortunate enough to have worked with him has been an inspiration to all who knew this talented and passionate musician. The title is drawn from one of his favorite places, the south shore of Massachusetts.

South Shore Soliloquy was commissioned by the PSC/PSU Band Alumni, Plymouth State University, Plymouth, New Hampshire.

INSTRUMENTATION

- 1 — Conductor Score
- 10 — Flute
- 2 — Oboe
- 2 — Bassoon
- 6 — 1st B♭ Clarinet
- 6 — 2nd B♭ Clarinet
- 2 — B♭ Bass Clarinet
- 2 — 1st E♭ Alto Saxophone
- 2 — 2nd E♭ Alto Saxophone
- 2 — B♭ Tenor Saxophone
- 1 — E♭ Baritone Saxophone
- 4 — 1st B♭ Trumpet
- 4 — 2nd B♭ Trumpet
- 2 — F Horn
- 3 — 1st Trombone
- 3 — 2nd Trombone
- 2 — Euphonium
- 1 — Euphonium T.C.
- 4 — Tuba

Percussion – 4 players:
- 1 — Bells
- 3 — Percussion (Suspended Cymbal, Bass Drum/Triangle)
- 1 — Timpani

SUPPLEMENTAL and WORLD PARTS
available for download from www.alfred.com/supplemental

E♭ Alto Clarinet
E♭ Contra Alto Clarinet
B♭ Contra Bass Clarinet
E♭ Horn
1st Trombone in B♭ T.C.
2nd Trombone in B♭ T.C.
1st Trombone in B♭ B.C.
2nd Trombone in B♭ B.C.
Euphonium in B♭ B.C.
Tuba in B♭ T.C.
Tuba in B♭ B.C.
Tuba in E♭ T.C.
Tuba in E♭ B.C.
String Bass

Alfred

Please note: Our band and orchestra music is collated by an automatic high-speed system. The enclosed parts are now sorted by page count, rather than score order.

Commissioned by PSC/PSU Band Alumni,
in memory of Dr. Gary Corcoran, Plymouth State University, Plymouth, New Hampshire

South Shore Soliloquy

FULL SCORE
Duration - 3:45

By Robert Sheldon
Op. 228

rall.
Fl.
Ob.
Bsn.
Cls.
B. Cl.
A. Saxes.
T. Sax.
Bar. Sax.
rall.
Tpts.
Hn.
Tbns.
Euph.
Tuba
(w/hard rubber mallets)
Bells
Sus. Cym.
Perc.
(w/med soft mallets)
Timp.
f
p
mp
7
8
9
10
11
12

13 a tempo
div.
Fl.
Ob.
Bsn.
Cls.
B. Cl.
A. Saxes.
T. Sax.
Bar. Sax.
Tpts.
Hn.
Tbns.
Euph.
Tuba
Bells
Perc.
Timp.
p
mp
13
14
15
16
17
18

21
Fl.
Ob.
Bsn.
Cls.
1
2
B. Cl.
A. Saxes.
1
2
T. Sax.
Bar. Sax.
21
Tpts.
1
2
Hn.
Tbns.
1
2
Euph.
Tuba
Bells
Perc.
Timp.
mp
mf
p
19
20
21
22
23
24
25

6

33 Poco più mosso ♩ = 80
Fl.
Ob.
Bsn.
Cls.
B. Cl.
A. Saxes.
T. Sax.
Bar. Sax.
33 Poco più mosso ♩ = 80
Solo
Tpts.
Hn.
(Alto Sax. 1)
(Alto Sax. 2)
(Tenor Sax.)
(Bass Cl.)
Play
Tbns.
Euph.
Tuba
Bells
Trgl.
Perc.
Timp.
33
34
35
36
37
38

poco accel.
41 Freely ♩ = 92
Fl.
Ob.
Bsn.
Cls.
B. Cl.
A. Saxes.
T. Sax.
Bar. Sax.
poco accel.
41 Freely ♩ = 92
Tpts.
Hn.
Tbns.
Euph.
Tuba
Bells
Perc.
Timp.
39
40
41
42
43
44

molto rall.
Fl.
Ob.
Bsn.
Cls.
B. Cl.
A. Saxes.
T. Sax.
Bar. Sax.
Tutti
molto rall.
Tpts.
Hn.
Tbns.
Euph.
Tuba
Bells
Perc.
Timp.
45
46
47
48
49
50

51 With hope ♩ = 80
div.
Fl.
Ob.
Bsn.
Cls. 1
Cls. 2
B. Cl.
A. Saxes. 1
A. Saxes. 2
T. Sax.
Bar. Sax.
51 With hope ♩ = 80
Tpts. 1
Tpts. 2
Hn.
Tbns. 1
Tbns. 2
Euph.
Tuba
Bells
Perc.
Timp.
mp
mf
p
51
52
53
54
55
56

rall.
59 Tempo primo ♩ = 72
Fl.
Ob.
Bsn.
Cls. 1 2
B. Cl.
A. Saxes. 1 2
T. Sax.
Bar. Sax.
rall.
59 Tempo primo ♩ = 72
Tpts. 1 2
Hn.
Tbns. 1 2
Euph.
Solo
Tutti
Tuba
Bells
Perc.
Timp.
p
mf
mp
cresc.
57
58
59
60
61
62

rall.
Larghetto ♩ = 60
div.
Fl.
Ob.
Bsn.
Cls.
B. Cl.
A. Saxes.
T. Sax.
Bar. Sax.
rall.
Larghetto ♩ = 60
Tpts.
Hn.
Tbns.
Euph.
Tuba
Bells
Solo
Perc.
Timp.
63
64
65
66
67
68
69